MY FIRST SPANISH PICTURE BOOK
CHILDREN'S LEARN SPANISH BOOKS

BABY PROFESSOR
EDUCATION KIDS

Speedy Publishing LLC

40 E. Main St. #1156

Newark, DE 19711

www.speedypublishing.com

Copyright 2016

All Rights reserved. No part of this book may be reproduced or used in any way or form or by any means whether electronic or mechanical, this means that you cannot record or photocopy any material ideas or tips that are provided in this book

LET'S KNOW MORE ABOUT SPANISH

NAME THAT PIC!
SPANISH CULTURE AND TRADITION

Shade the box and rewrite the correct answer

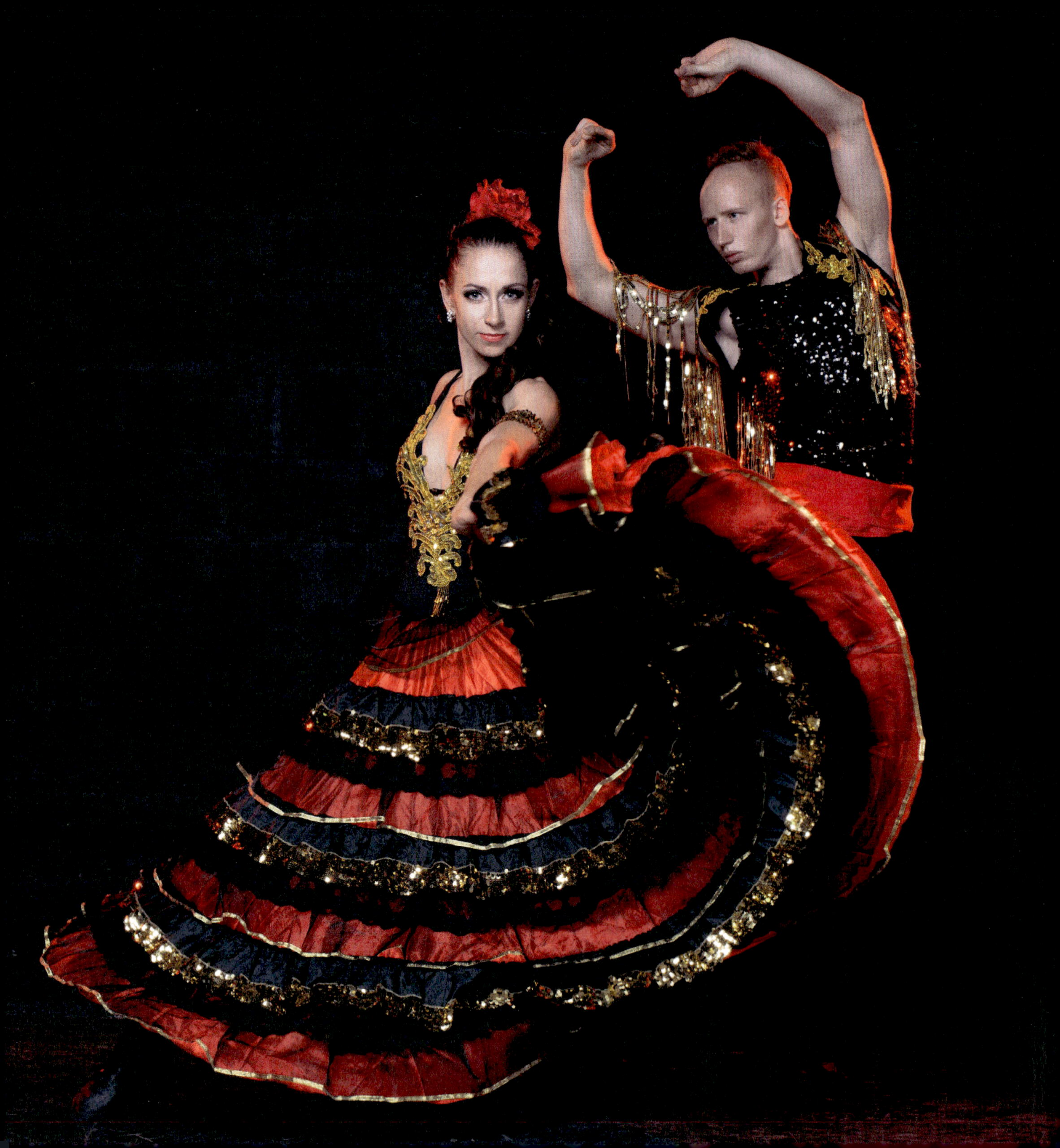

FLAMENCO

BULLFIGHT

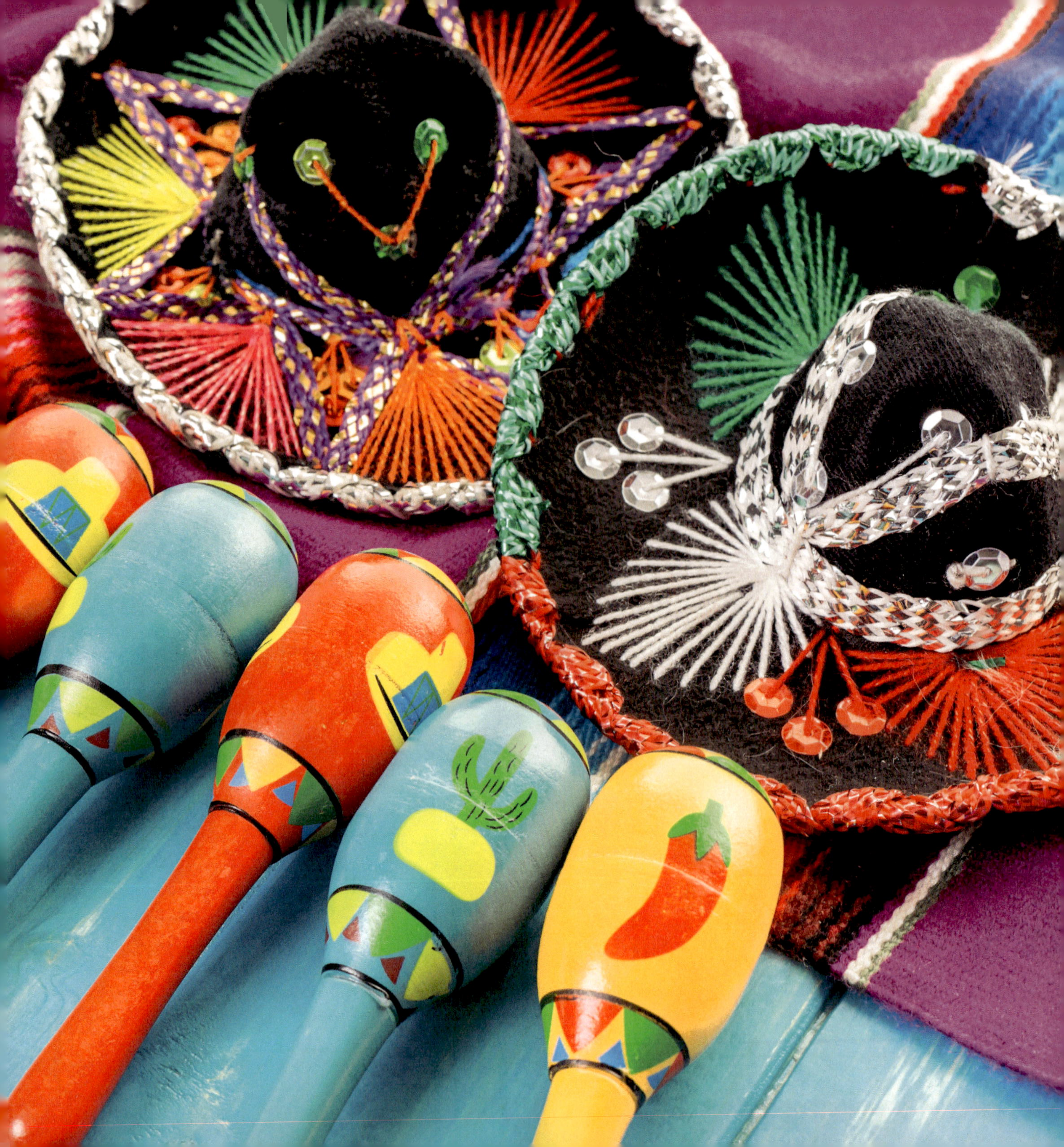

FIESTA

party

SIESTA

nap

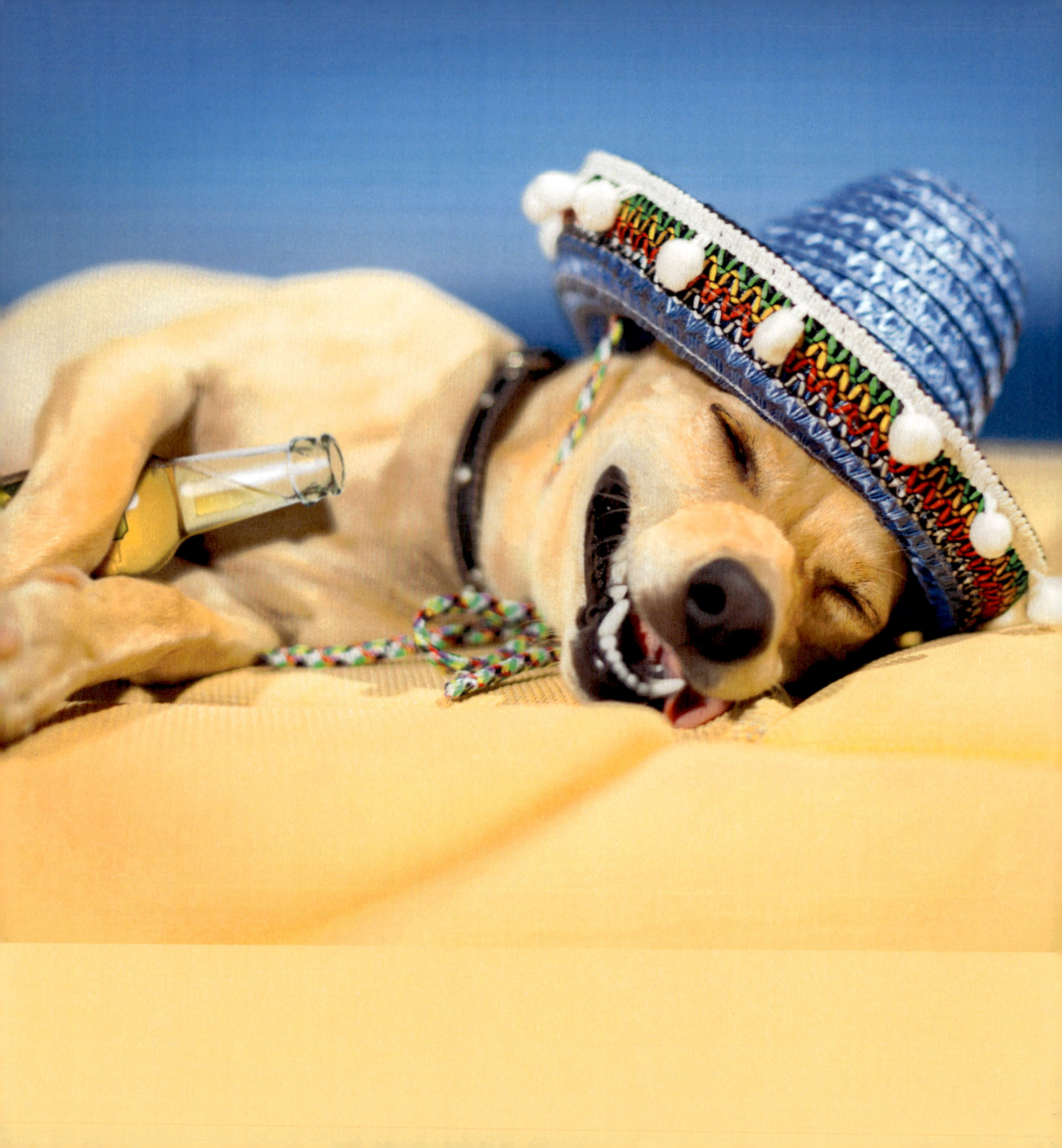

SIESTA

BULLFIGHT

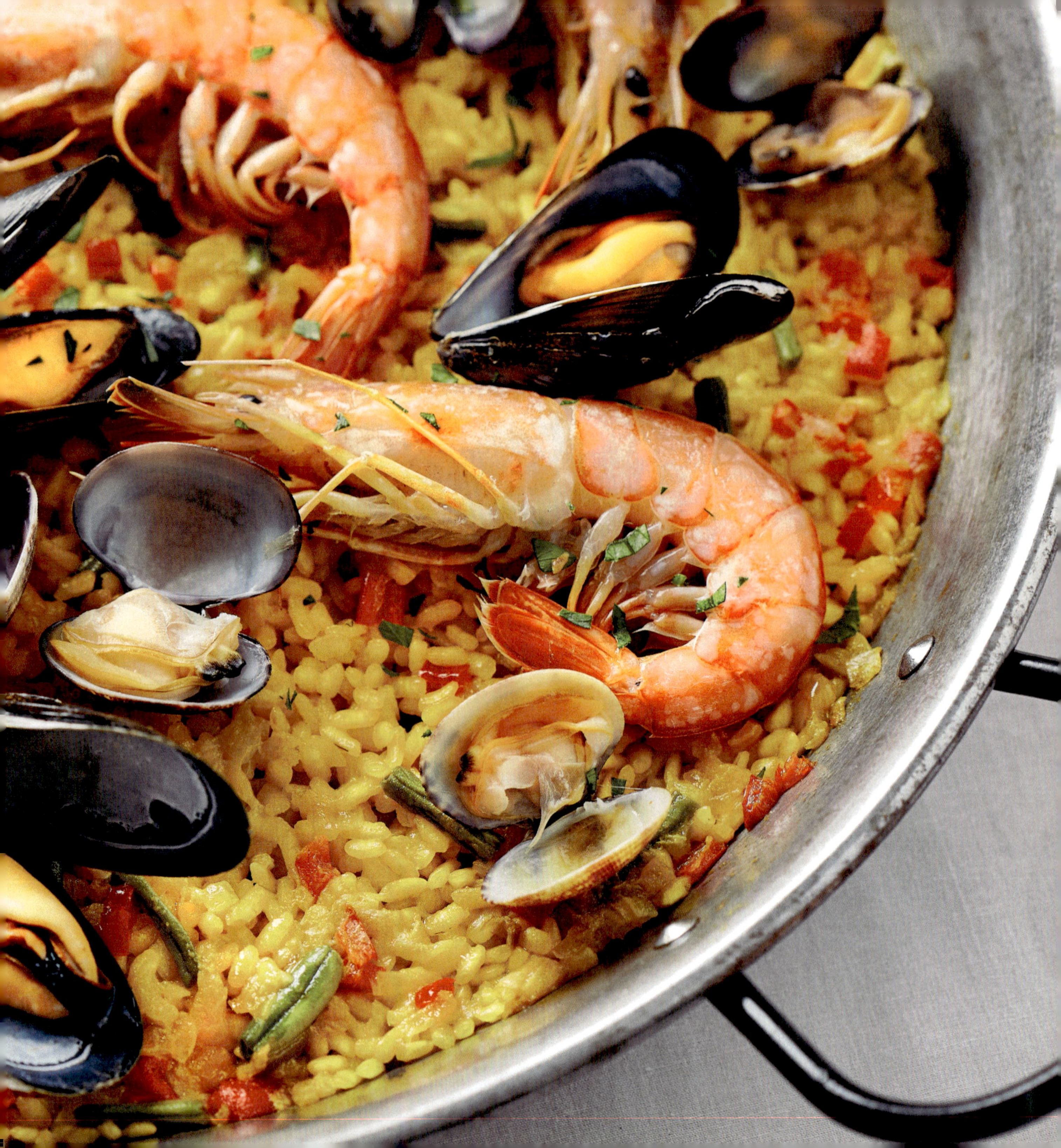

PAELLA

BULLFIGHT

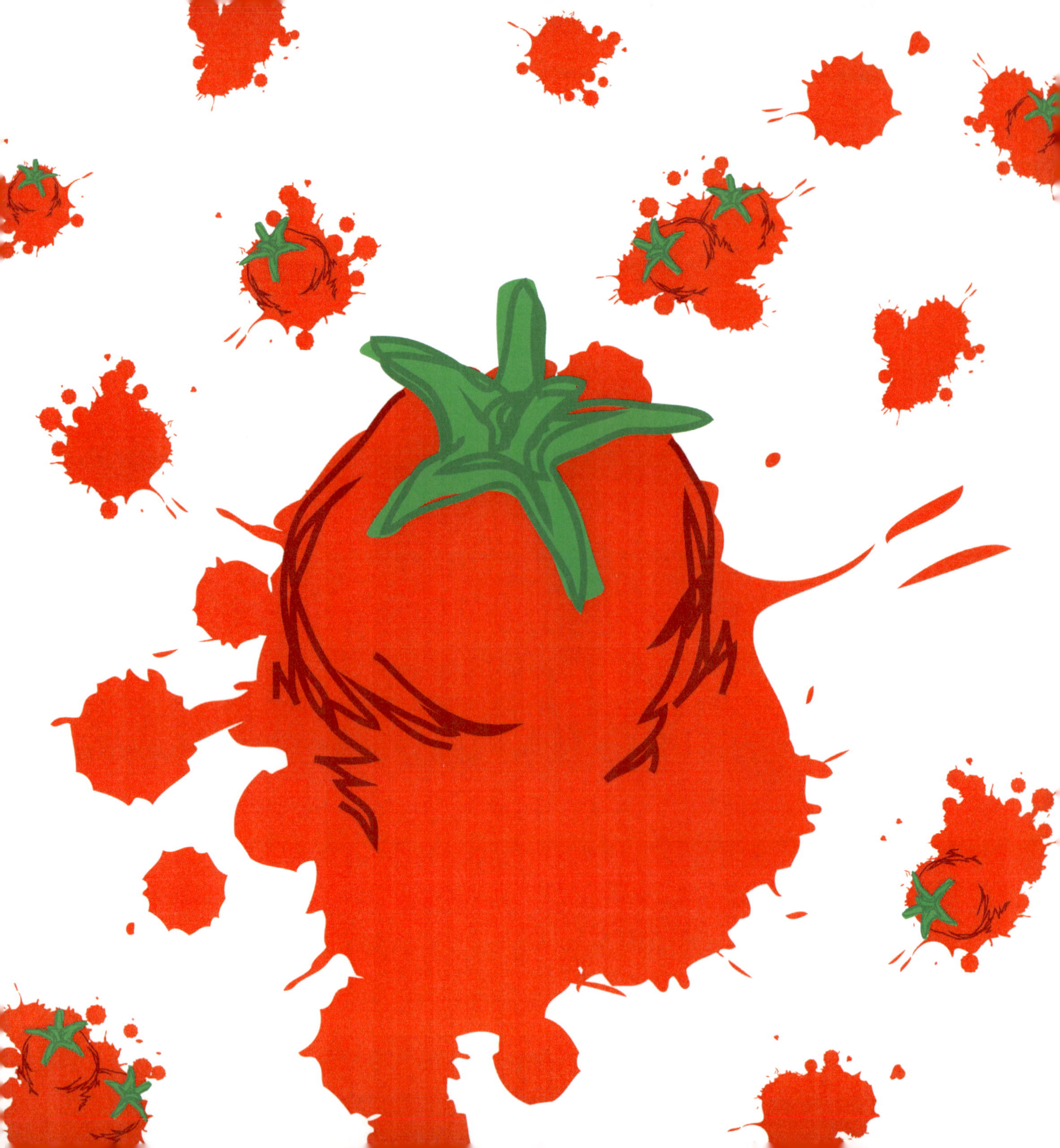

PAELLA

LA TOMATINA

tomato

GUESS THAT PIC!
SPANISH VOCABULARY

Shade the box and rewrite the correct answer.

Write also the english term for the incorrect answer.

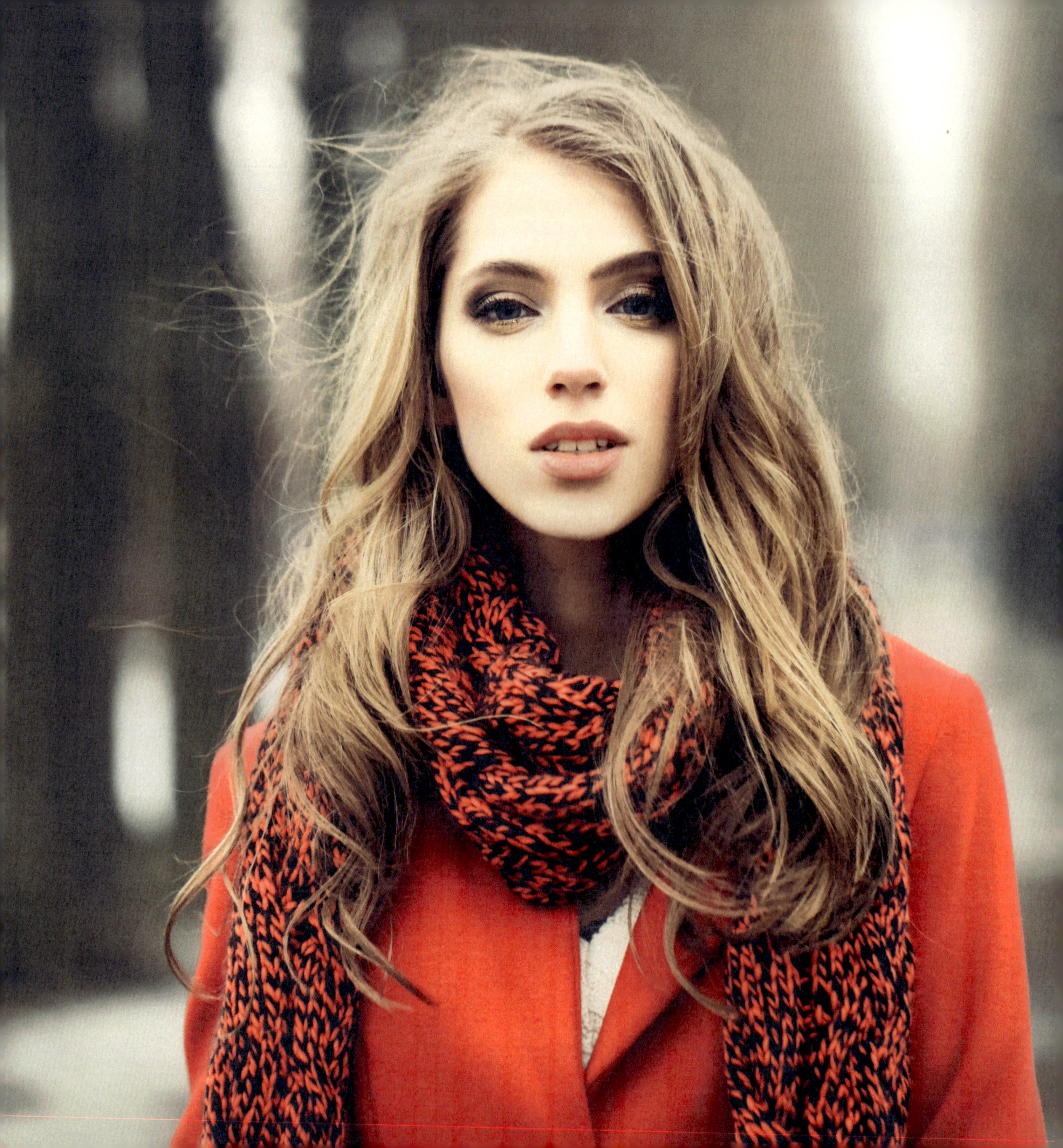

MUJER

Write the English term here:

woman

GRACIAS

Write the English term here:

thank you

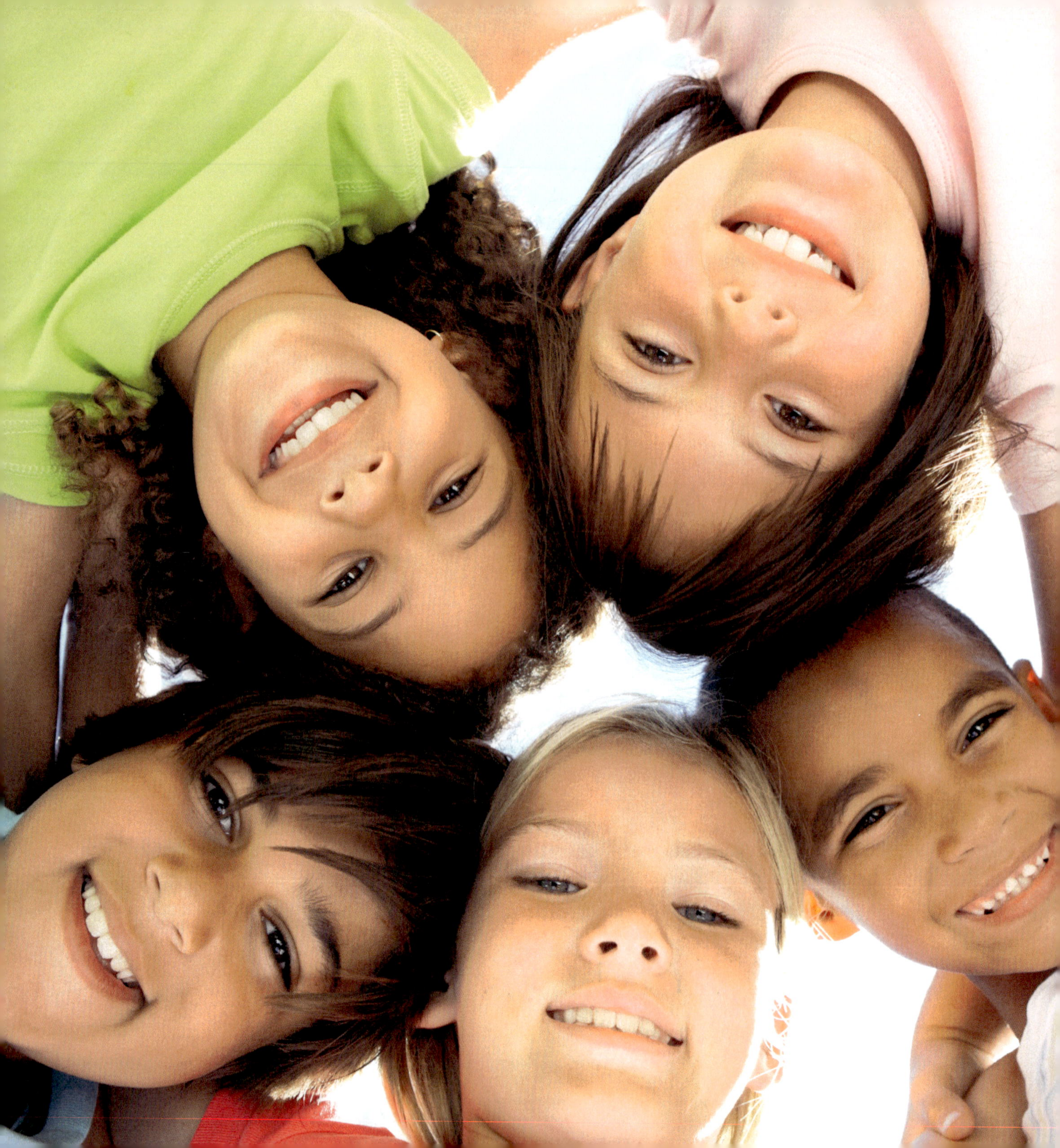

DONDE

Write the English term here:

where

AMIGO

Write the English term here:

friend

Thank you

BUENO

Write the English term here:

good

GRACIAS

Write the English term here:

thank you

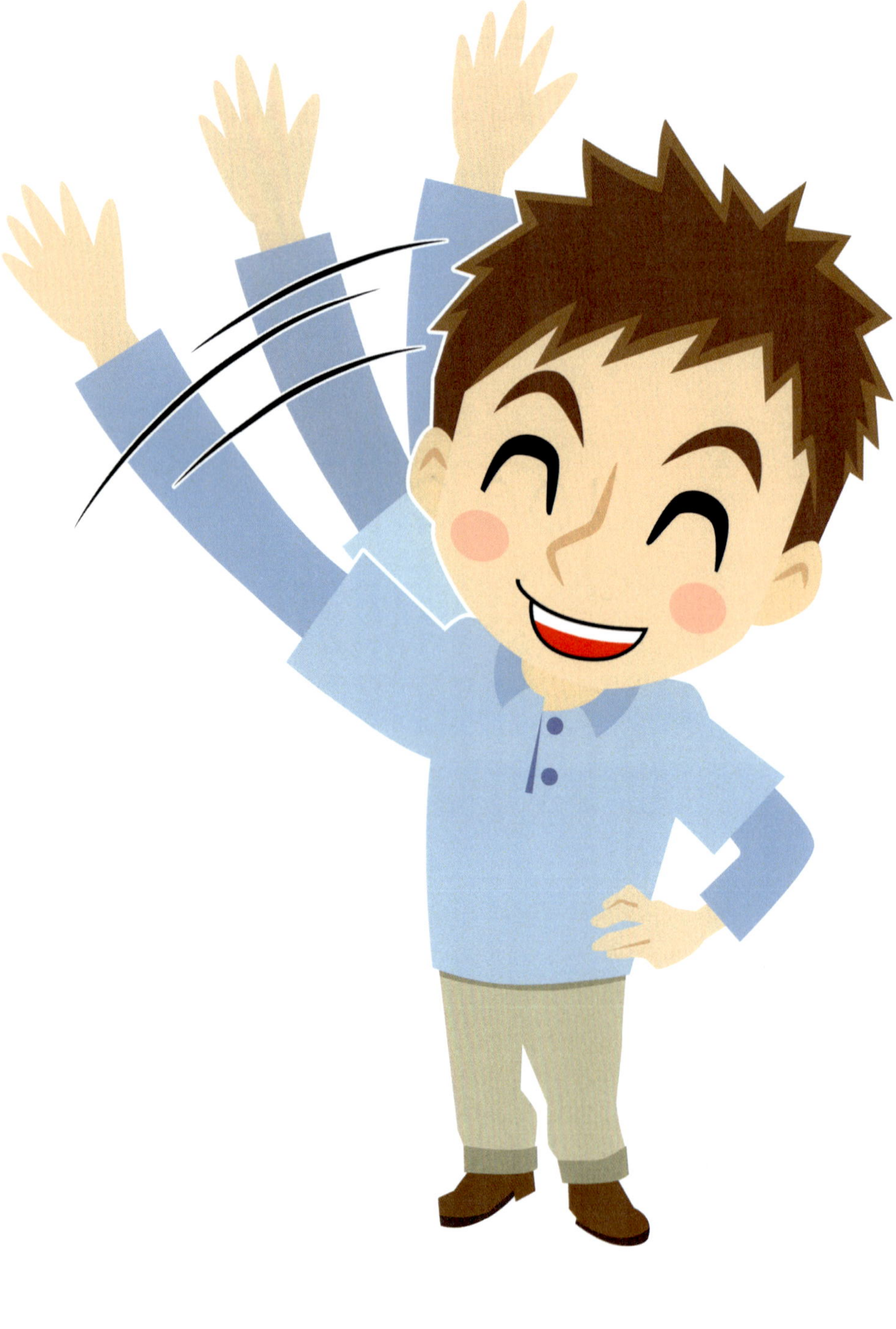

ADIÓS

Write the English term here:

bye

BEBER

Write the English term here:

drink

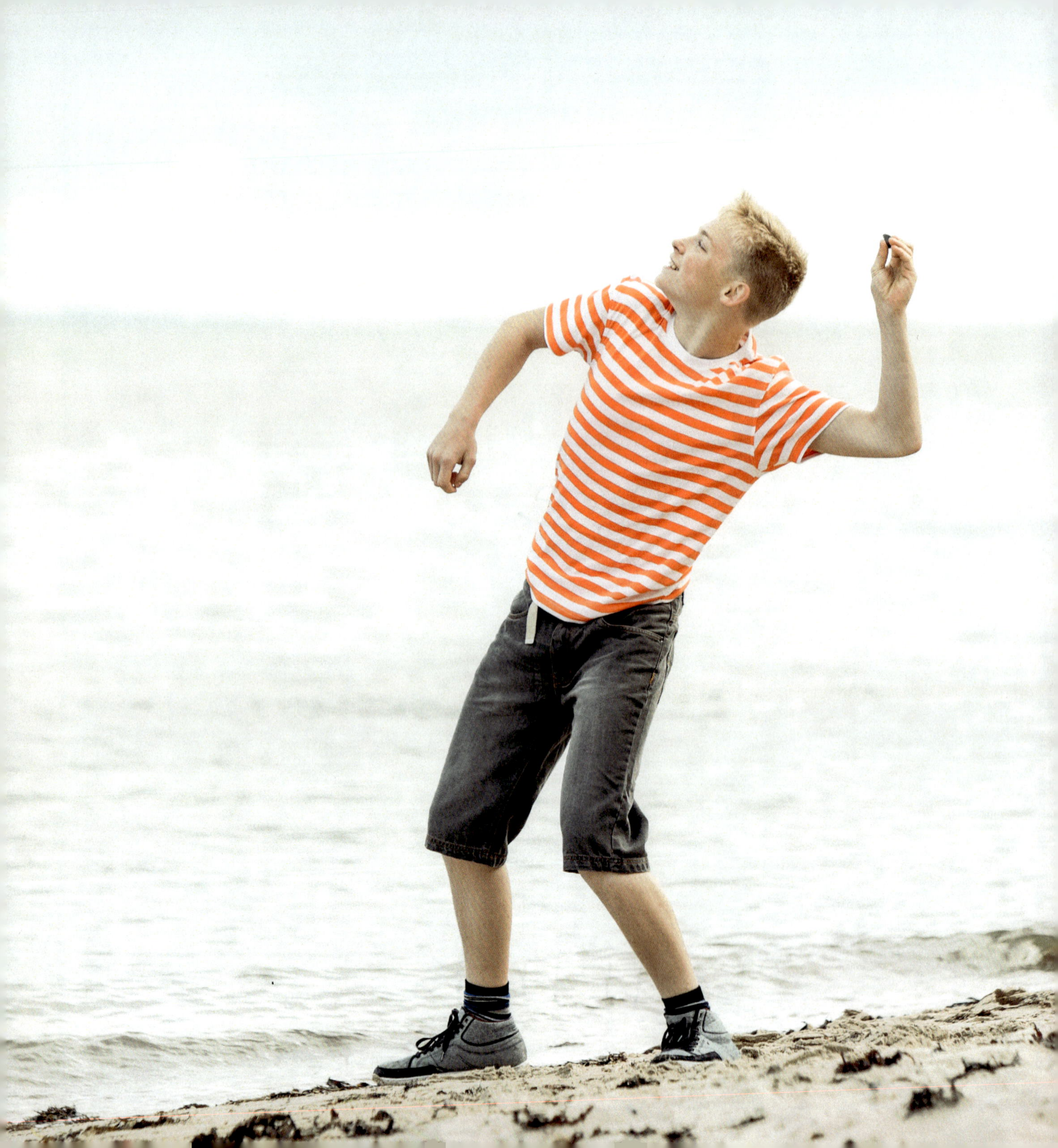

TAMBIÉN

Write the English term here:

also

ECHAR

Write the English term here:

throw

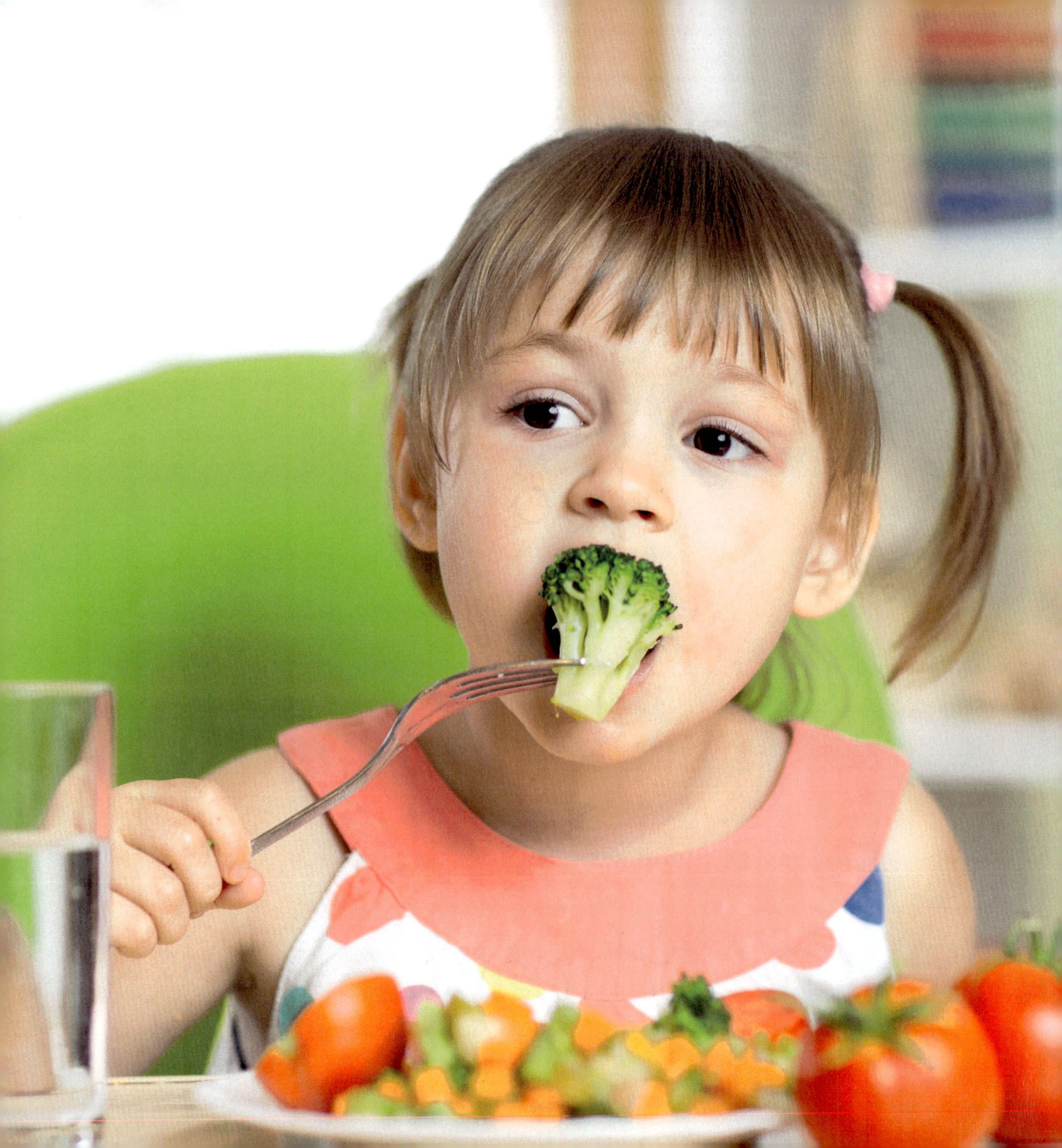

BUENO

Write the English term here:

good

COMER

Write the English term here:

eat

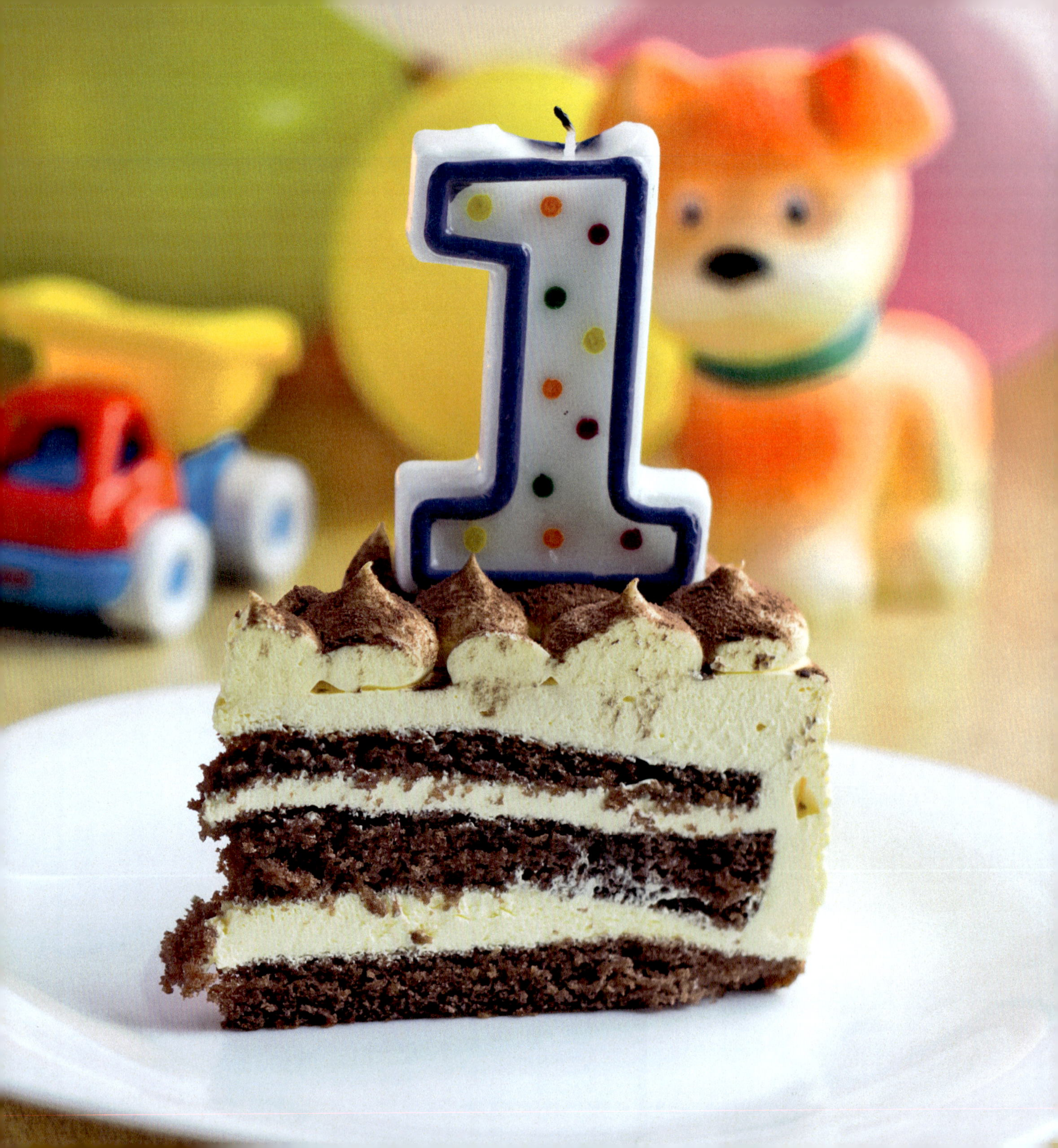

PRIMERO

Write the English term here:

first

COSA

Write the English term here:

thing

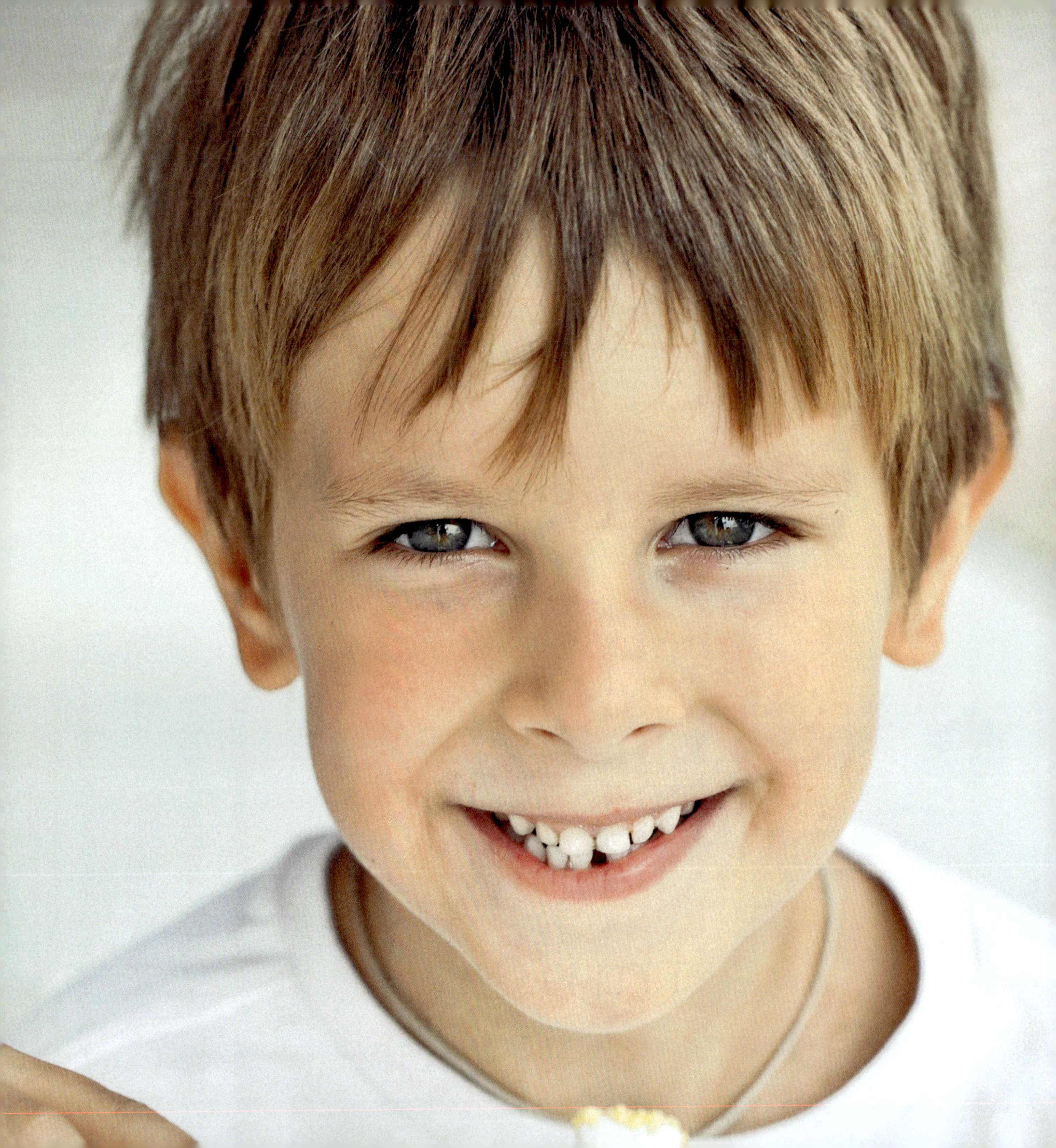

TRISTE

Write the English term here:

sad

FELIZ

Write the English term here:

happy

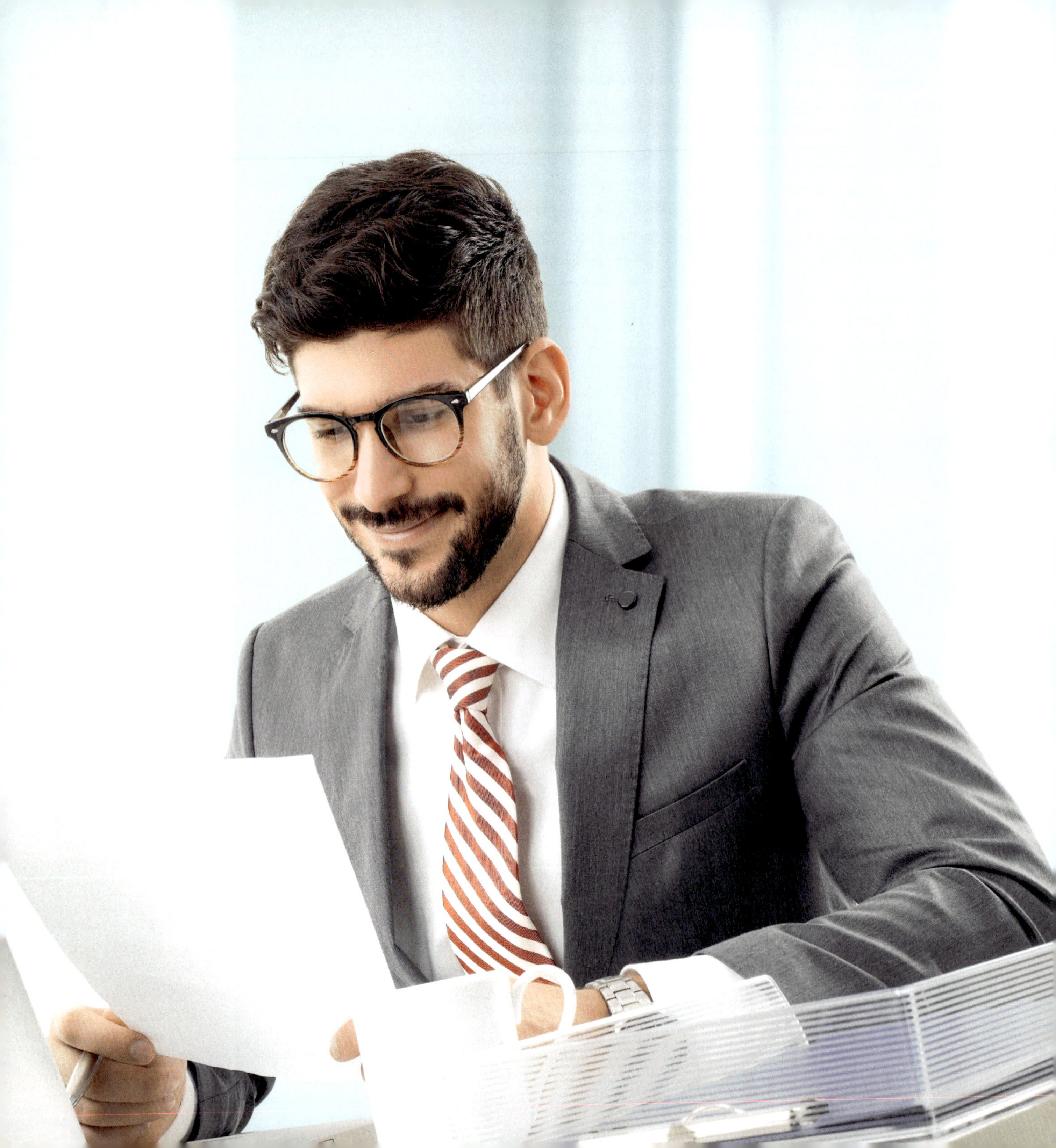

HOMBRE

Write the English term here:

man

ENCONTRAR

Write the English term here:

find

ANSWER KEY

FLAMENCO

FIESTA

SIESTA

PAELLA

LA TOMATINA

Shade the box and rewrite the correct answer.

Write also the english term for the incorrect answer.

MUJER

Write the English term here:
Woman

GRACIAS

Write the English term here:
Thank you

GUESS THAT PIC!
SPANISH VOCABULARY

DONDE
Write the English term here:
Where

AMIGO
Write the English term here:
Friends

BUENO
Write the English term here:
Good

GRACIAS
Write the English term here:
Thank you

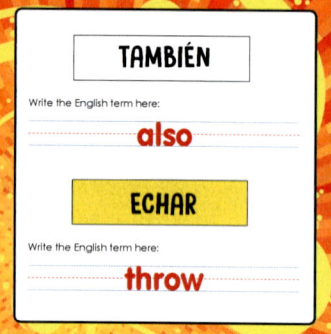

ADIÓS
Write the English term here:
goodbye

BEBER
Write the English term here:
drink

TAMBIÉN
Write the English term here:
also

ECHAR
Write the English term here:
throw

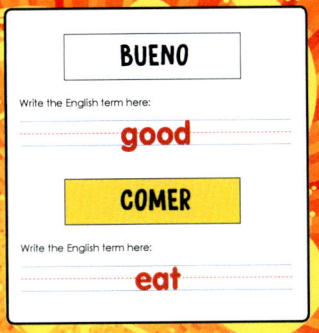

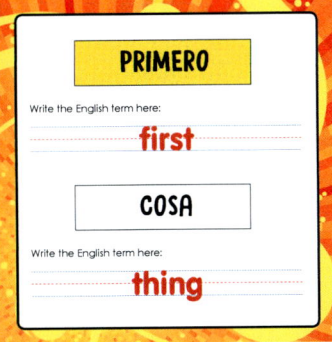

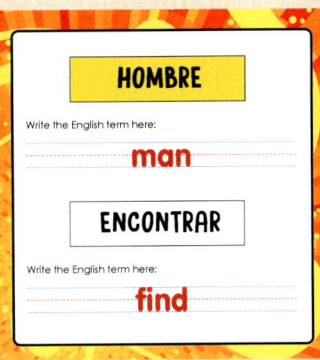

Spanish	English
BUENO	good
COMER	eat
TRISTE	sad
FELIZ	happy
PRIMERO	first
COSA	thing
HOMBRE	man
ENCONTRAR	find

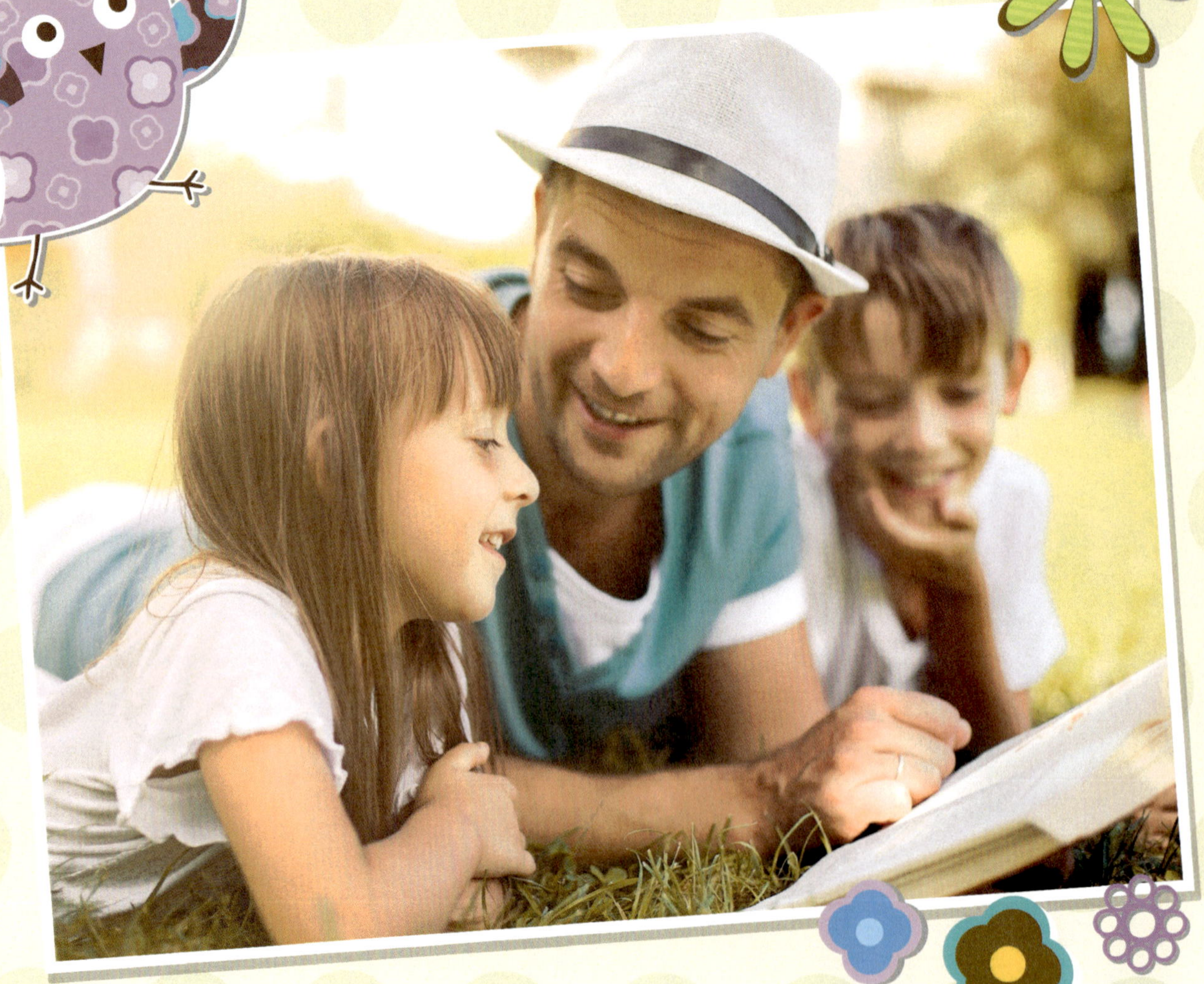

Visit

BABY PROFESSOR
EDUCATION KIDS

www.BabyProfessorBooks.com

to download Free Baby Professor eBooks and view our catalog of new and exciting Children's Books

Made in the USA
Middletown, DE
25 August 2017